Speak Texan
in 30 Minutes or Less

By Lou Hudson

T H E   T E X A S   T W A N G
P R E S E R V A T I O N   S O C I E T Y

EVERT CARTER, CHIEF ELOCUTIONIST
© BARRY SHLACHTER, TOP HAND
DISTRIBUTED BY THE GREAT TEXAS LINE
P.O. BOX 11105, FORT WORTH, TEXAS 76110
TEL: (800) 73TEXAS

For Starters

"I dearly love the state of Texas, but I consider that a harmless perversion on my part, and discuss it only with consenting adults."
– *Texas columnist Molly Ivins*

Imagine you've arrived in Waxahachie, Alvarado or Mexia, and can't even pronounce the name of the town, let alone understand the answer to "Where's the best barbecue around?"

Imagine your embarrassment when your new Texas neighbor or host or family member speaks to you, and you cannot understand what they are saying.

You can feign deafness and perhaps get out of a momentarily sticky situation, but what about the next time?

Fortunately, you are holding in your very hands the answer to your dilemma (are you deaf or are you ignorant?)

Speak Texan in 30 Minutes or Less can make you understandable to Texans and able to understand any Texan, no matter where in the world y'all may be.

There; you have just learned your first Texan word: Y'all, a sometimes-collective noun meaning the both of you, or all of you, or just you by yourself, depending on the situation.

It is simple to add to this word to greatly enlarge your Texan vocabulary.

For instance: Y'all etyet? (Have you folks eaten?)

Y'all fixinta dainz? (You folks going dancing?).

How y'allbin? (How have you - singular in this case - been doing?)

See? It's easy, if you just know how. And this book will show you how, in an easy-to-master style. Read it and learn.

Read this book, and if you don't sound like a Texan, you might could just understand one, at least.

And remember, you can always tell a Texan. (You just can't tell 'em much).

CHAPTER 1
The Great Divide

"If you've ever driven across Texas, you know how different one area of the state can be from another. Take El Paso. It looks as much like Dallas as I look like Jack Nicklaus."
– *Pro Golfer Lee Trevino*

First, some geographical caveats:

Texas is so big, it has at least two distinct dialects: the East Texas drawl and the West Texas twang.

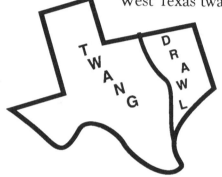

The drawl is characterized by a slow elongation to words, usually adding a syllable (for instance: ma'am comes out MAY-am; help becomes HAY-yelp.)

The twang, on the other hand, is more nasal and sometimes shortens words: Mam, Hep..

When you are in the middle of Texas, you may have problems deciding which to utilize in your quest for information.

And you must always be careful not to get your twang caught in your drawls.

Twangit Dangit!

Here are some examples of drawlspeak:

ArREYust: To be apprehended by the constabulary.

BAWul: Round thing, often thrown.

HAYur: Stuff on your head

MAWul: Big thing, with shops and eating places. Teen-age girls, especially, love to hang out in them.

WEEyun: Opposite of lose.

Now some twangspeak:

Bobwar: Fencing medium with sharp points scattered throughout, designed to keep cattle in (or out). Also known as the devil's rope.

Gummit: The national, state or local operating authority, often made up of executive, judicial and legislative branches. Also used as part of an invective: Dad-gummit.

Shurf: Head law enforcement official in most Texas counties.

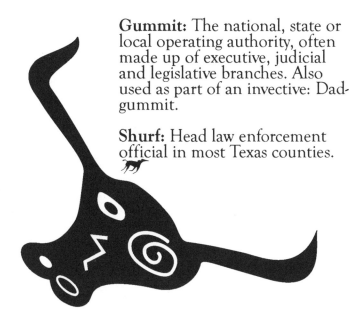

YOU MIGHT BE A TEXAN IF ...
SOMEONE YOU KNOW HAS
USED A FOOTBALL SCHEDULE
TO PLAN THEIR WEDDING DATE.

YOU DO WANT A TEXAN
TO SAY YOU'RE ...
HAPPY AS A GOPHER
IN SOFT DIRT.

YOU DON'T WANT A TEXAN
TO SAY YOU'RE ...
OLDER THAN TWO TREES.

YOU DO WANT A TEXAN
TO SAY ...
YOU'LL DO TO RUN
THE RIVER WITH.

CHAPTER 2

Gray-yam-er

"There's a lot of uncertainty
that's not clear in my mind."
– *Former Texas House Speaker Gib Lewis*

Most words are accented on the first syllable in Texas, and they often will have one more syllable than they do in other regions (in drawlspeak, anyway).

Occasionally, though, the opposite is true, as in HEP (a request for assistance).

However, even HEP is also sometimes subject to the rule, if pronounced by a Texas beauty queen:

HAYulp
CAWwur (automobile)
CAYut (feline)
DAWug (canine)
FIEyure (blaze)
SHEoot (see)
guh-HALL-leeee (expression of
    great surprise)
HEyum (a male person)
KAyuff (baby bovine)
PEEugh (porcine)
Rurnt (ruined)
 SHEoot (to fire a gun)
WAYell (hole dug for water or
    oil)

As a start, in East Texas, if you encounter a word you've never heard before, apply these simple rules:

    1. If there's a Y sound, take it out. That will allow you to figure out many words, and will often also change a word from drawlspeak to twang.

    2. Change any AY sound to an EH sound.

    3. See if there's a way to cut out a syllable. (Run the syllables together and see what you get). 🐆

YOU MIGHT BE A TEXAN IF
... YOU HAVE OWNED AT LEAST
ONE BELT BUCKLE BIGGER
THAN YOUR FIST.

YOU DON'T WANT A TEXAN
TO SAY YOU'RE ...
DUMBER THAN DIRT.

YOU DO WANT A TEXAN TO
SAY YOU'RE ...
WOLVERINE MEAN.
(THIS IS ACTUALLY
A COMPLIMENT...
USUALLY).

CHAPTER 3

Sounds Like

"Despite the fact that certain features of Texas dialects of English are sometimes stigmatized by speakers from other areas as hicky or `incorrect,' Texans will continue to use them, partly because people who live in Texas wish to distinguish themselves from other Americans."
– *Keith Walters, University of Texas linguist*

Texas pronunciations are not necessarily phonetic.

The Pedernales River, the bucolic stream running through the ranch of the late President Lyndon Baines Johnson, is pronounced PERD-nal-is, for example.

Mexia, the Central Texas hometown of Anna Nicole Smith, is Ma-HAY-uh.

A traveling couple were once passing through that small town south of Dallas and arguing over its pronunciation.

"MEX-ee-ah," said the man.

"Ma-HAY-uh," said the woman.

"All right," said the man, "we'll settle this," turning into a fast-food joint.

Walking in the door, he called to a waitress, "How do you pronounce this place?"

She called back, slowly, so he could understand properly: "D-A-I-R-Y Q-U-E-E-E-N."

Speaking of which, if you want to conduct serious business in Texas, you must do it at a Dairy Queen.

Fortunes are made and lost in these Texas icons of fast food and there isn't a small town in the state that doesn't transact important matters there.

Major problems, such as world peace, the national debt, cattle prices, the economy, foreign policy and why the Dallas Cowboys are not in the Super Bowl, are solved there over coffee every morning, often by otherwise anonymous men with graying hair, face stubble, a bit of bare paunch extending over the belt buckle, and as often as not, a cowboy hat or a gimme cap from the local feed store.

YOU MIGHT BE A TEXAN IF ...
YOU CAN PROPERLY
PRONOUNCE THE NAMES OF
THE TOWNS MEXIA, LAMESA,
BOERNE AND MESQUITE.

YOU DON'T WANT A TEXAN
TO SAY YOU'RE ...
UGLY AS A MUD FENCE.

YOU DO WANT A TEXAN
TO SAY YOU'RE ...
AS HANDY AS HIP
POCKETS ON A HOG.
(I.E., YOU'RE PRETTY NEAT).

CHAPTER 4

Texanacity

"Real Texans do not use the word
`summer' as a verb."
— Texas commentator Molly Ivins

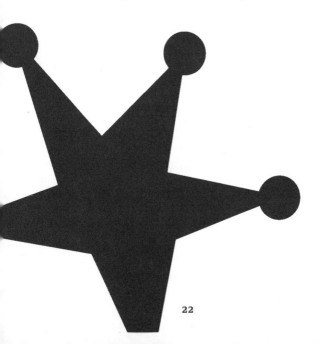

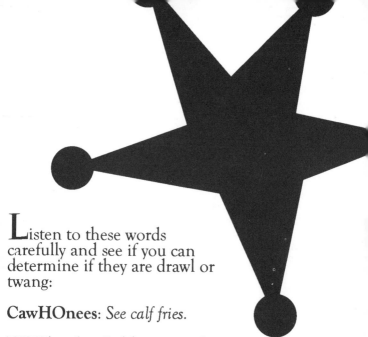

Listen to these words carefully and see if you can determine if they are drawl or twang:

CawHOnees: *See calf fries.*

EYESbawks: Cold storage place where things are kept so they won't get spoilt.

GEYut: To fetch something. Often used as a command to dogs, as in "Gone boy-e, go geyut it."

HEREyar: Handing something to someone (*"HEREyar, tayuk the-us dollar beeyul and go GEYut us a sodypop"*)

LIMOseen: (1). a cattle breed. (2). a new pickup with an extended cab.

SPAY-uhl. Passage of time. (*"Come sit a SPAY-uhl and take a load off"*).

WhurYAT: A query as to someone's location.

YAWNTo: A query: *YAWNTo go to the MAWul?*

(NOTE: Do not confuse this with the admonition "YAWTo," as in "YAWTo put them aigs in the EYESbawks 'fore they GEYut spoilt." It is the opposite of ``YAWn't,'' as in ``YAWn't leave them aigs out on the sink or they'll get spoilt."

Twangit Dangit!

More on pronunciation:

In Texan, any word ending in "ing" leaves the "g" silent, as in fixin' to, goin' to, weavin' around, walkin' and ridin', etc.

One problem with speaking Texan is, you can't speak it anywhere else in the world, unless of course you are conversing with another Texan.

A Texas journalist, after taking Russian lessons for a spayuhl, went to work for a news service in Moscow.

One day, he was trying to reach a contact at the British Embassy and initially spoke Russian to the operator who answered the phone.

Quickly determining that she spoke English, he switched to his native tounge, fully flavored with the West Texan twang he developed growning up in Abilene.

After a
momentary
pause, the
operator
asked, "Excuse me
sir, would you resume
speaking in Russian. I
can't understand your
English."

YOU MIGHT BE A TEXAN IF ...
YOU'VE EVER BEEN
EXCUSED FROM SCHOOL
BECAUSE "THE COWS GOT OUT"

YOU DON'T WANT A TEXAN
TO SAY YOU'RE ...
ALL HAT AND NO CATTLE
(A PERSON WHO IS ALL TALK
AND NO SUBSTANCE).

YOU DO WANT A TEXAN
TO SAY YOU'RE ...
QUICK AS A HICCUP.

CHAPTER 5

Ya'll get it?

"Texans are, with rare exception, proud of their identity as Texans, a fact that is reflected in their speech."
– *Keith Walters, University of Texas linguist*

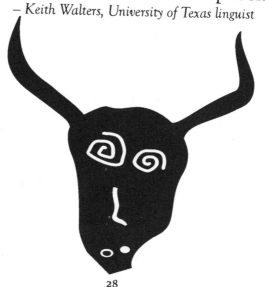

A helpful definition:
Calf fries: How to tell the difference between calf fries and chicken nuggets (and why you should care):

A reporter was attending the annual media feed at Fort Worth's Southwestern Exposition and Livestock Show and Rodeo some time ago, and declared that on the buffet table were the best-tasting chicken nuggets she had ever eaten.

She did not stop to consider why they would be serving chicken at a promotion for a show that celebrates beef.

The chicken nuggets were not chicken after all (well, chicken-fried steak isn't chicken, either, so big deal), but that Texas delicacy known as calf fries. (They are called a delicacy because the subject must be approached delicately).

They are, to put it delicately, what's mainly left over when a young bull is transformed into a young steer.

The Spanish term is *cojones* (Pronounced cawHOnees). Look it up.

They also are known, for unknown reasons, as mountain oysters.

First clue: Chicken nuggets are rarely spherical.

Second clue: You can't cut chicken nuggets with a fork (you may not be able to cut calf fries this way; it depends on the original disposition of the bull.).

Third clue: People around you will rarely, if ever, snicker when you bite into a chicken nugget.

Victuals: This is the actual way to properly spell the word that is traditionally pronounced Vittles. It means, simply, food.

★

Since Texas is, according to one state agency, a "whole other country," it has holidays no one else has and not everyone can pronounce:

San Jacinto Day [Sand JAH-sent-TOE], April 21, marking Gen. Sam Houston's decisive 1836 victory over Mexico's Gen. Santa Anna, securing Texas' independence.

Cinco de Mayo [SINK-KOE de-MY-OH], marking the May 5, 1862, routing of superior French forces from Pueblo, Mexico. Holiday celebrations are led by Hispanic communities but can be enjoyed by anyone.

Juneteenth [JOON-teenth], marking the belated announcement to African-American slaves in Texas on June 19, 1865, that they were made free by the defeat of Confederate forces in the Civil War. Celebrations marking the anniversary have now spread nationwide.

Diez y Seis de Septiembre [Dee
es ee SAYCE deh sep-tem-bray
– anniversary of the September 16,
1810 start of Mexico's struggle for
independence from Spain. Hence,
this day is similar in many ways to the
American 4th of July. As a large part
of the Texas population is Hispanic,
this is a widely observed holiday.

Texas
Independence
Day, marking the
March 2, 1836,
signing of the
declaration of
independence
from   Mexico.

YOU MIGHT BE A TEXAN IF ...
YOU USE THE PHRASE "FIXIN TO"
ALMOST DAILY.

YOU DON'T WANT A TEXAN
TO SAY YOU'RE ...
UGLY AS HOMEMADE SOAP.

YOU DO WANT A TEXAN
TO SAY YOU'RE ...
CUTE AS A POSSUM.
(A WORD OF WARNING HERE: THIS
IS NOT TO BE USED BY A MALE
ADDRESSING A MALE. WELL,
PERHAPS SOME OF YOU COULD ....)

CHAPTER 6
Texanitions

You dance with them that brung ya.
— *An old Texas expression of loyalty*

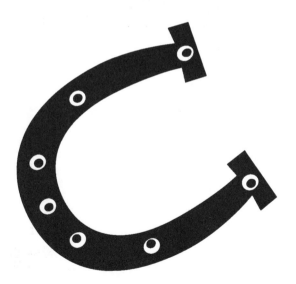

ila —

Thought you
might get a
kick out of
this — Phoebe
probably knows
it all!

Yvette

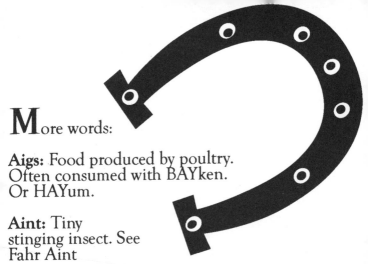

More words:

Aigs: Food produced by poultry. Often consumed with BAYken. Or HAYum.

Aint: Tiny stinging insect. See Fahr Aint

BAYken: Pork breakfast meat, usually consumed with Aigs

B.L.: A man's first name, as in former President B.L. Clinton.

DAINce: To move rhythmically to music.

Dinner: This can be either the noon meal or the evening meal, which is also known as supper.

Fahr: Produced by flames; sometimes used in expression of surprise, as in SHEoot Fahr! FIEyure in drawlspeak.

FawHEETuhs: A Texas staple (and invention), will appear as Fajitas on your menu. Texans, you must remember, are rich in Spanish heritage and use the language frequently.

Fahr Aint: Particularly nettlesome Aint, characterized by massive swarming when disturbed. Please note that these are imported nuisances, not to be confused with our more genteel domestic Fahr Aints, which have only two teeth instead of three and are much gentler in their attacking swarms.

Fixins: Food. Also known as vittles.

Fixinto: Action is forthcoming shortly.
Used on a Nike t-shirt, it would read `` I'm fixinto just do it."

GAHyus: Another petroleum product, often used in heaters. A liquid by the same name powers internal-combustion engines.

Heighty: Form of greeting, as in, "Heighty, howyawldoin?"

Hep: To give assistance, as in "Kinihepyew?" *(see)* *Twangspeak.* Or, HAYulp: East Texas or beauty queen variation.

How'syamomandthem? (Is your family doing well?)

Jeet: To consume food, as in "Heighty, jeetyet?"

Kinihepyew: Asking some one if they need assistance.

NAWrth: Opposite direction from south. Where Yankees come from. Often used with the prefix UP.

Oyal *(rhymes with royal)***:** Black petroleum compound extracted from the ground, as in oyal wayell. Or Twang vairation, Awl wayl.

PuhKAHN: the nut spelled pecan, and it's not PEE-can.

ROE-dee-oh: where ropers and buldoggers compete, and definitely not, roe-DAY-oh.

Tuhrst: Suicide bomber or other insurgent.

Whomped: Slapped upside the head, usually by your momma.

Ya'll: Group of people, although can also be used with as few as one as in "Ya'llcomeback, heah?"

Yew: Pronoun, often used in expressions of gratitude, as in, "Thank yew for a lovly evenin, ma'am."

'Zbarbecue, Bar-B-Q, barbey-que.

IMPORTANT CULTURAL NOTE:

If you wish to be a Texan of any stripe, or simply want to experience some of the best vittles anywhere, you have to eat barbecue, and it has to be beef, not that stringy pork stuff they serve farther Up Nawrth.

And to appreciate the cuisine fully, you also must obtain a recording of Robert Earl Keen's paean to the delicacy, *Barbecue*.

It's also a necessity to fully appreciate Big Red strawberry drink.

You should also obtain a copy of Keen's *Merry Christmas from the Family*, which has nothing to do, or not much anyway, with barbecue, but may or may not help you to understand Texans a little better. Probably not. But singing portions of it will impress your new neighbors if you've just moved to the state.

So, to order barbecue properly, you need to consider the type of establishment you are in. If it's a small out-of-the-way joint, not part of a chain, you simply bellow:

"Gimmie a sliced with onion."

And that's it. Or, if you wish to appear more debonair: "A sliced with onion, poreFAYvor".

The Big Red is automatic. (If you have to have some other drink, such as an iced tea or, heaven forbid, a Coke ~ the only thing more unTexan would be a Vanilla Coke ~ you can order that, but you will be frowned upon. at .

A Dr Pepper is an acceptable substitute, but they probably won't even serve coffee, and if they do, it will be made with three-day old grounds (which in some locations is a plus) and they will laugh at you impolitely if you ask for cream.

A Lone Star, Pearl or Shiner beer is also acceptable, and drunk from the longneck.

If you fetch your barbecue at a non-Texas- based chain restaurant, shame on you. Angelo's in Fort Worth is permitted simply because of its history and ambiance, but the fire code prohibits them from having a sawdust floor anymore - pity.) *D Magazine* likes a place called Peggy Sue Barbecue in Dallas.

But you don't need to search those places out. Just look around for the nearest little rundown-looking building with a faded BBQ sign and check it out.

Some of the best barbecue can be found in little mom-and-pop storefronts that may be 50 years old and apparently in need of everything.

But if you sniff and it smells wonderful, head on in.

The mothers of all barbecue joints are in Lockhart. not far from Austin; some don't even provide utensils with your meal. The scrumptious feast is served on butcher paper, allowing you to savor the last drop of flavor simply by licking your fingers.

And remember, chili is the State Dish of Texas and contains no beans. Beans is a separate dish. 🐎

YOU MIGHT BE A TEXAN IF ...
YOU KNOW EXACTLY WHAT
CALF FRIES ARE AND
EAT THEM ANYWAY.

YOU DON'T WANT A TEXAN
TO SAY YOU'RE ...
TIGHTER THAN BARK ON A TREE
(I.E., STINGY).

YOU DO WANT A TEXAN
TO SAY YOU'RE ...
BIG ENOUGH TO HUNT BEAR
WITH A SWITCH.
(NOTE: THIS CAN ALSO BE
SOMETHING YOU DON'T
WANT A TEXAN TO SAY OF YOU;
GENERALLY, THOUGH, IT
REFERS TO SIZE OF HEART
OR INTENT OR DEDICATION, NOT
SIZE OF PHYSIQUE.)

CHAPTER 7

Tradin' with Texans

Avoid doing bidness
with people
who are as greasy as
fried lard.

Buying a ranch in Texas doesn't take much ~ just find one you like, shake hands with the owner and pony up several million dollars. Or several hundred million, depending on the size.

Ranching in Texas has fallen victim to the same problems as operations elsewhere ~ rising land prices, lower cattle prices and climate fluctuations ~ only on a much bigger scale.

In West Texas, it may take as many as 10 acres to support one cow, and there's nothing else the land is good for, except near Amarillo, where one rancher has planted Cadillacs.

On horses:

There is a uncommon bond between Texans and horseflesh, and lots of Texans have horses.

The Dallas-Fort Worth region, for instance, has more horses per capita than any similarly-size area in the country, maybe the world.

Horses are not animals, or pets, or possessions, or collateral, or chattel property, or material goods in Texas.

They are family and are treated as such, maybe better. Just look at the barns some of them live in. They're nicer than your home.

At a spread in Mansfield, Texas, where part of the movie *North Dallas Forty* was filmed, visitors have often headed first to the barn when they drive up, the main house being hidden somewhat by the location.

The barn is big, it is fancy and it is rich. The horses are sleek, they are well fed, they are well conditioned, they are well trained, they are quite spoiled. Treat them with deference, or they will place you on the social blacklist.

One pronunciation note: The animal is known as a hoss.

Technically, a young male horse is a colt and a young female horse is a filly, and a young horse generically is a foal; but in Texas, if it's a young horse, it's a colt, period. In Texas, a filly is a young woman. 🐎

49

CHAPTER 8
Gettin' around

"Newcomers to the state inevitably pick up such traditional Southernisms as y'all. Those who are not already from the South sometimes begin saying fixin' to and might could as the natives do. In this way, language enables Texans, native or naturalized, to identify themselves as such. "

– *Keith Walters, University of Texas linguist*

Helpful phrases, in English, then in Texan translation:

"Sir, can you direct me to the nearest restroom?"
"Pardner, kin yew show me to the 2-holer?"

"May I have a Dr Pepper?"
"Kin yew whup me up a little sody pop, pour FAYvore?"

(Note, ``pour fayvore'' is derived from the Spanish, but it has become part of the culture, and Texans will readily understand it. Also note that "sody pop" will nearly always get you a Dr Pepper in most areas of the state, unless you are being served by a newly arrived Yankee; but in

Central Texas and some other smaller regions, you may get a Big Red instead.

"Hello, have you eaten? Care to have a bite?
"Heighty, jeetyet? Comeon. Let's mosey to the chuck wagun."

"What do you call this in Texan?
"Little lady, whut's this?"

"Is that correct?"
"No bull?" (In unpolite company, you may add the second half of the word).

"I don't understand"
"Huh?"

"Hurry up!"
"Scoot!"

"Where can we go dancing?"
  "Whur's the nearest honky-tonk?"

  "I'm not feeling well"
  "Ahm feelin' poorly."
(To which the reply may be, "You do look
a little peak-ed.")

  "Is there a bus to the airport?"
  "Pardner, kin I hitch a ride to th' airport?"

  "Can you fix a flat?"
  *"Pardner, my wheel's flat on one side; kin
      yew plug it up?"*

  "Is there a nightclub show here?"
  "Whut time does Willie Nelson come on?"

More notable town names, pronounced just as they appear, of course:

Boerne (BERnie)

Chihuahua (CheeWAHwah) *Never mind that Paul Harvey once broadcast it as ChaHUAhua.*

Refugio (Ree-FURE-eeo)

Waxahachie (WAUX-ah-HATCHee)

Palestine (PAL-is-teen)

Gruene (GREEN)

Llano (LAN-oh)

De Kalb (deeCAB)

Dimmit (Dimmit)

Mesquite (MESkeet)

Lamesa (LaMEEsa)

Sipe Springs (SEEP Springs)

Buda (BYOO-duh)

Burnet (BURN-it)

DeLeon (DEE-lee-on)

Some Texas towns are conjoined, as in Bruceville-Eddy and Wilmer-Hutchins, wherein two towns or school districts have merged, often for economic reasons. Besides, they are conversation-starters.

Interestingly, in the case of Bruceville-Eddy, it even spreads into two counties, making it (them?) Bruceville-Eddy in McLennan-Falls counties.

A warning: Always identify the county a particular city goes with, because there may be more than one town with the same name in Texas.

There are, for instance, at least two Parkers, six Oak Groves, two Mountain Springs and three Mountain Views, two Mozells (but only one Mozo), two Piney Points (plus one Piney Point Village), seven Pleasant Groves and four Pleasant Hills, four Pleasant Valleys, a couple of Pleasure Points and no less than three Punkin Centers.

There are six River Oaks
, six Royal Oaks and four
Salems. Five Silver Citys, two
Simpsonvilles,

There is only one Friendly, but seven
Friendships. There are five Four Corners (which
makes 20), plus Four Points and Four
Way. Five Lone Stars.

The champion appears to be
Midway, of which there are at least 18,
according to the Texas Almanac. (And
there are 14 Fairviews).

There is an Addielou, a Bess, a Bettie and a
Beulah. A Donna and a Dot. A Peggy, a Fairy, a
Percilla, a Lovelady, a Loving and a
Louise.

There is a Pflugerville (which
once had the nation's longest running high
school football winning
streak), a Phalba and a
Pharr. There's a
Sprinkle, a Dime
Box, a New
Dime Box, and a
Gun Barrel City.

There is a Timber Lake and a
Timberlake, a Timber Lake Acres and
two Timber Lake Estates. A Tomball
and a Tom Bean. A Todd Mission
and a Todd City. Toledo Beach and
two Toledo Villages. Bee Cave, Bee
House and Beeville. Zipperlandville
and Zippville.

There is a Round Rock and a
Carl's Corner. A Coffee City and a
Coffeeville. Cold Spring, Coldsprings
and Cold Water. A Dam B (but no
Dam A).

Ding Dong is, of course, in Bell County. There is a Frog and a Frognot. A Hoop and a Holler (that's one name). A Joy and a Jolly (that's two names).

A Kokomo and a Kona Kai. A Monkeyville and a Monkstown.

There is a North Zulch (but no Zulch). A Pluck and a Plum.

There are even two Santa Annas, same name as the generalissimo who defeated the Texians at the Alamo (but was in turn defeated by Gen. Sam Houston's forces).

AND YOU MIGHT BE A TEXAN IF ...
YOU HAVE EVER HAD THIS
CONVERSATION:
"YOU WANNA COKE?"
"YEAH."
"WHAT KIND?"
"DR PEPPER."

YOU DON'T WANT A TEXAN
TO SAY YOU ...
DON'T KNOW WHETHER TO SCRATCH
YOUR WATCH OR WIND YOUR BUTT.

YOU DO WANT A TEXAN
TO SAY YOU'RE ...
TOUGH AS AN OLD BOOT.

CHAPTER 9

Weather or not

Texas has four seasons: Drought, flood, blizzard and twister.
– Old Texas Saying

Texas Weather (always spelled with a Capital "W.")

There are enough stories about Texas Weather to fill a book. And in fact, there have been several, including *Texas Weather* by George Bomar and another by the same name by Harold Taft.

Texas is quite possibly the only place on Earth that can hit you with tornadoes, record heat, hurricanes, blizzards, dust storms, earthquakes, hailstorms, wind storms, thunderstorms, lightning storms, ball lightning, St. Elmo's Fire, ice storms, drought, floods, tidal waves, water spouts, swarms of tumbleweeds and mosquitoes, noseeums, locusts, fire ants and killer bees.

Sometimes all on the same weekend. And with the most beautiful sunset you've ever seen.

And at times, rain is not just scarce, "It's so dry, the trees are bribing the dogs."

As folklorist J. Frank Dobie wrote, "One Texas claim is that it doesn't have a climate, just weather."

YOU MIGHT BE A TEXAN IF ...
WHEN YOU HEAR A TORNADO SIREN,
YOU GO OUTSIDE AND LOOK FOR A
FUNNEL CLOUD.

YOU DON'T WANT A TEXAN
TO SAY YOU'D ...
GRIPE IF YOU WAS GOING
TO BE HUNG WITH A
BRAND-NEW ROPE.

YOU DO WANT A TEXAN
TO SAY YOU'RE ...
SWEET AS SORGHUM.
OR
YOU CLEAN UP GOOD
(USUALLY BEFORE A DATE)

CHAPTER 10
The Rules

"There's nothing in the middle of the road
except a yellow stripe and a dead armadillo."
— *Anonymous Texan quoted by Jim Hightower*

One does NOT wear a straw cowboy hat to a wedding. Or a funeral (it could turn into your own). Or in the winter. Or to a fancy dress ball.

One wears a silver belly (light gray) with a Peter Bros. crease.

One can wear a straw hat in the summer or to a square dance. Or the State Fair. Or the Fort Worth Stock Show (but not the final Grand Champion Steer sale).

Boots are to be worn at all times, but not the same pair.

Ropers are for, well, roping.

There are riding cowboy boots and dress cowboy boots.

And they are cowhide leather. Do not make the mistake of wearing exotic hides: alligator, snake, ostrich, water buffalo, goat, etc. Texans wear cowhide, period. It can be rough or smooth, tanned or dyed. But only cowhide.

You don't have to wear your boots to bed, but it's OK if you want to.

How to tell the difference between a fresh cow patty and a weathered cow patty:

Try to pick it up.

If you can, it's weathered.

If you can't, it's fresh. Don't step on it.

Wipe your hands on your jeans: Wranglers or Levi's if you're a male, Panhandle Slim or Wranglers if you're a female. If your jeans say something sissy like Gap or Calvin Klein, shame on you, and go back to where you came

from: I-35 and I-45 run north and south, I-20 and I-10 run east and west. Take your pick.

Don't ask people you meet if they are Texans. If they are, you'll know soon enough because they will tell you.

If they're not, you'll know soon enough because they won't tell you.

Don't tell an Aggie joke (comparable to Polish jokes up North) to an Aggie (a proud alum of Texas A&M University, a school near Snook), except:

What do you call an AGGIE 10 years after graduation?

Boss.

Let Aggies tell them, though. ("My favorite Aggie joke? I'm sorry I don't understand the question." ~ Singer Lyle Lovett, A&M class of '79)

Qrdering a beer in Texas is simple.

You say, "KinIhavabeer?"

You'll get a Lone Star, a Pearl, or a Shiner.

Rules for non-Texans (follow them and you (won't offend a Texan, and with practice, might could just pass as a Texan....)

1. Pull up your droopy pants.

2. Texans drive pickups because they need to. It's called a "gravel road." No matter how slow you drive, you're going to get dust on your Lexus. Drive it or get out of the way.

3. They may smell like pigs, cattle and oil wells to you. They smell like money to Texans.

4. You may be proud of that $60,000 car you drive. Texans aren't impressed. They have quarter-million-dollar cotton strippers they drive 3 weeks a year.

5. You meet a vehicle coming the other way on a two-lane road, you wave. It's called being friendly.

6. If your cell phone rings while a bunch of doves are comin' in, a Texan likely will shoot it out of your hand. Hope it isn't at your ear at the time.

7. Texans eat catfish and crawdads. You want sushi and caviar? They have 'em at the bait shop.

8. The "Opener" refers to the first day of deer season. It's a religious holiday held the closest Saturday to the first of November.

9. Texas men open doors for women. That is applied to everyone, regardless of age. Has nothing to do with equality of the sexes. Has to do with gettin' whomped by your momma if you don't, regardless of your age.

10. There is no "vegetarian special" on most menus in Texas. You order steak. Order it rare. Or, you can order the Chef's Salad and pick off the 2 pounds of ham & turkey.

11. Friday night during high school football season is another sacred holiday.

12. Final reminder: Sam Houston once said, "Texas could get along without the United States, but the United States cannot, except at great hazard, exist without Texas."

YOU MIGHT BE A TEXAN IF ...
YOU AREN'T SURPRISED TO FIND
MOVIE RENTALS, AMMUNITION,
CHEWING TOBACCO AND BAIT
IN THE SAME STORE.

YOU DON'T WANT A TEXAN
TO SAY YOU'RE ...
DUMB AS A BOX OF HAMMERS.

YOU DO WANT A TEXAN
TO SAY YOU ...
KNOW YOUR MANNERS LIKE
YOUR MOMMA TAUGHT YOU.

CHAPTER 11

Advanced Texaspeak

"Looks like he sorts bobcats for a living."
—Texan description of a person who looks,
well, somewhat disheveled.

All swole up: Aggravated, obstinate, proud or self-absorbed.

Clabber up and make down: A weather condition having the appearance of fixin' to come a frog-strangler. *See gully washer.*

Come hell or high water. *(Used by a person who will do what he/she says, count on it).*

Common mutt-horse *(see plug ugly)*

Dang-nab it: Expression of disappointment or disgust, as in "shucks," or "oh, heck" or "shoot fahr."

Gully-washer: Plumb big rainfall. Also known as a frog-strangler.

Blue norther: Really bad cold front. They are Characterized by dark blue northern horizon with hard north wind, occasionally blizzard conditions. In West Texas, can be mixed with dust.

Pole-axed: Knocked down. Clobbered.

Whomper-jawed: Out of kilter, off-balance, not fitting properly. "Hidden in the basement like a crazy aunt."

Blacker than midnight under a skillet: Very dark.

Fine as frog's hair: *(Ever seen hair on a frog? That's REALLY fine).*

Like the dogs was after him: Being in a big hurry.

Colder than a well-digger's lunch pail (or butt): Plumb cold.

Tend to your own knittin' (or rat killin'): Mind your own business.

That's telling him how the cow ate the cabbage! "You go girl!"

∩ ∩ ∩

Evil thoughts are like chickens – they always come home to roost.

When I say frog, you say, "How high ya'll want me to jump?"

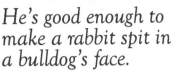

He's good enough to make a rabbit spit in a bulldog's face.

This ain't my first rodeo: I've done this before.

That dog won't hunt: That's a bunch of bull; *a favorite expression of former Texas Gov. Ann Richards, who is as Texan as they come.*

Don't squat with your spurs on.

Emotional and physical states in Texas:

Like a one-legged man at a butt-kicking contest:
A person not very coordinated, not very successful.

Like a gnat in a hailstorm:
Helpless.

Having a hissy fit and stomping on it: A condition to be avoided.

Rode hard and put up wet: 1. Being really tired, pooped, looking exhausted. 2. A slutty-looking woman.

Beaten like a rented mule: Looking exhausted.

Half a bubble outta plumb: Not quite all there.

YOU MIGHT BE A TEXAN IF ...
YOU THINK A LUXURY CAR
IS A CHEVY Z-71 4X4 PICKUP
WITH AN EXTENDED CAB.

YOU DON'T WANT A TEXAN
TO SAY YOU'RE ...
CROOKED AS A DOG'S HIND LEG.

YOU DO WANT A TEXAN
TO SAY YOU'RE ...
SPIT SHINED AND
ALL POLISHED UP.

Lou Hudson is a fourth-generation Texan whose Lone Star family roots trace back to the 1850s. The Fort Worth native attended the University of Texas at Arlington, beginning when it was still Arlington State College, a part of the Texas A&M system. Forced to become a writer because Yankees could not understand his speech, Hudson spent 35 years reporting and editing for the *Fort Worth Star-Telegram*.

(Sources: Rice.edu, Welsh Realty Inc., Berlitz, The Book of Texas Wisdom, Texas Almanac, The Handbook of Texas Online, assorted anonymous e-mails and unidentified Internet contributions, and more than six decades of being a Texan.)